A Crabtree Branches Book

ANCIENT
WARRIORS

BRUTAL
SPARTANS

Thomas Kingsley Troupe

Crabtree Publishing
crabtreebooks.com

School-to-Home Support for Caregivers and Teachers

This high-interest book is designed to motivate striving students with engaging topics while building fluency, vocabulary, and an interest in reading. Here are a few questions and activities to help the reader build upon his or her comprehension skills.

Before Reading:
- *What do I think this book is about?*
- *What do I know about this topic?*
- *What do I want to learn about this topic?*
- *Why am I reading this book?*

During Reading:
- *I wonder why...*
- *I'm curious to know...*
- *How is this like something I already know?*
- *What have I learned so far?*

After Reading:
- *What was the author trying to teach me?*
- *What are some details?*
- *How did the photographs and captions help me understand more?*
- *Read the book again and look for the vocabulary words.*
- *What questions do I still have?*

Extension Activities:
- *What was your favorite part of the book? Write a paragraph on it.*
- *Draw a picture of your favorite thing you learned from the book.*

TABLE OF CONTENTS

Facing the Enemy

The Spartan warriors stand shoulder to shoulder. Their helmets shine in the sun. They watch the enemy advance.

The Spartans raise their shields to form a wall. Spears are gripped tightly, ready to strike. They are **outnumbered** by thousands. Even so, the Spartans will stay and fight!

What's a Spartan?

Sparta was a warrior society in ancient Greece. It became a **city-state** after defeating the city-state of Athens in the Peloponnesian War (431-404 B.C.E.).

The people that lived in Sparta were known as Spartans. The soldiers that fought for Sparta were known as *hoplites*.

Fun Fact

Hoplite comes from the Greek word *ta hopla* which means tool or equipment.

A Spartan hoplite devoted his entire existence to fighting for Sparta. Nothing was more important to these soldiers. Not even family.

They fought many battles close to home, fighting over land and resources. Each victory made Sparta stronger. Spartan hoplites also defended Sparta against foreign enemies.

Spartan History & Life

Leonidas was the king of Sparta from 490 B.C.E. to 480 B.C.E. He was killed in battle by the Persian army in the Battle of Thermopylae.

His death was considered a heroic **sacrifice**. Leonidas and 300 of his hoplite warriors fought to defend their territory. Outnumbered by the Persians, all 300 were killed in battle.

Male citizens of Sparta were trained their entire lives for only one job. That job was to serve as a soldier in Sparta's military.

Spartan boys began their life as a soldier at age 7. They were entered into a harsh training program called the *agoge*. There they learned to fight, compete, and survive.

Fun Fact

A Spartan became a true soldier at age 20, after 13 years of training. He served for around 40 years. He could stop fighting at age 60.

Spartan Clothing

Spartan warriors wore a breastplate made of leather or bronze, called a cuirass, to protect their chest from attack. It was attached to another piece of armor to protect their back.

Strips of leather called *pteruges* were attached to the armor. They hung over the warriors' limbs to protect their arms and upper legs in battle.

A bronze helmet protected the soldier's head, face, and neck. The front of the helmet had a T-shape for their eyes, nose, and mouth. A crest on top sometimes held plumes or horse hair.

Fun Fact

The Spartan helmet crest made warriors seem taller to scare enemies. It might also have been a sign of wealth.

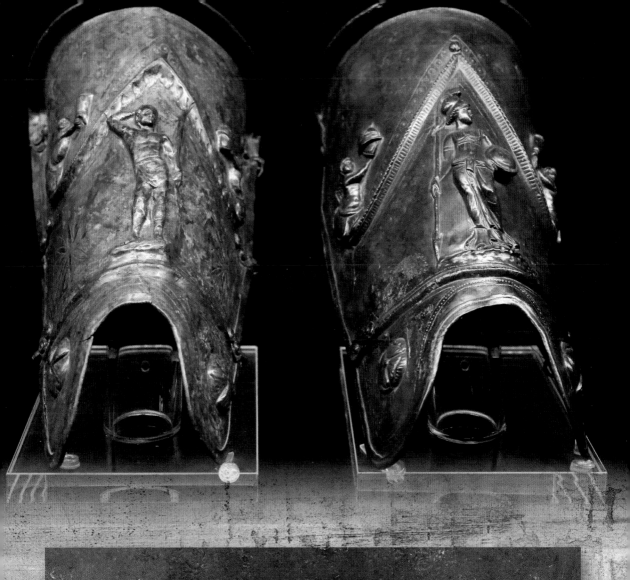

Bronze coverings called *greaves* protected the knees, shins, and legs. These were not attached to the rest of the armor. Greaves protected their legs, but let them move and fight freely.

Spartan Weapons

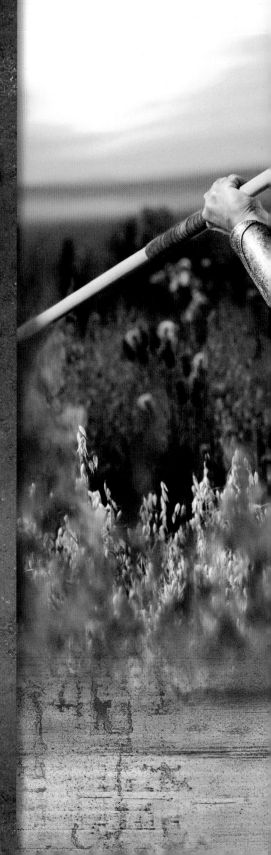

Hoplites carried only a few weapons with them onto the battlefield. The main weapon was a long, wooden spear, called a *doru*. It had a bronze or iron blade at the end.

Hoplites also carried a *machaira*, or short sword, for up-close battles. They also kept a dagger in case their main weapons were lost.

Fun Fact

The hoplite's spear was 7 to 9 feet (2.1 to 2.7 m) in length. It was used to keep an enemy away from the front lines and to attack from a distance.

In the other hand, the hoplite carried a large, round shield. Called a *hoplon* or an *aspis*, it was made of wood and covered with bronze.

Fun Fact

A hoplite's shield was big and heavy. It was nearly 3 feet (1 m) in diameter and weighed up to 18 pounds (8 kg)!

The shield often had different **emblems** on the front. Some displayed creatures from Greek **mythology**. Others had an upside-down V which stood for their region, Laconia.

Spartan Fighting

The Spartan soldiers were experts at combat on the battlefield. Using their large shields and long spears, they formed a barrier to protect the soldiers behind them.

The hoplites would line up in close formation with shields raised. They would crouch behind them with spears poking out between the shields. This was called a *phalanx* formation.

While in the phalanx formation, the hoplites could advance together. Their shields made a barrier that was hard to break through.

The formation would push toward the enemy. If the barrier was broken or **flanked**, the Spartans could fight with swords in close combat.

Spartans Today

Where have all the Spartan warriors gone? Sparta reached the height of its power in 404 B.C.E. After defeating Athens, the Spartans ruled with an iron fist. It did not stay peaceful for long.

The city-state of Sparta was never quite the same. Battles with neighboring nations weakened the once great nation.

Fun Fact

Decades before its downfall, earthquakes in 465 and 464 B.C.E. led to a slave **revolt** in Sparta. The conflict was so serious, Sparta needed to call on neighboring cities to help.

Even today, Spartan warriors are remembered as brave and strategic soldiers. Tales of their battles and combat style have been passed down through the ages.

We use the word Spartan today to describe a lack of comforts, or having a strict self-discipline and no fear of danger. Spartan soldiers will always be remembered as the strongest and most deadly ancient warriors!

Glossary

city-state (SIT-ee steyt) An area in Greece that had its own rulers and laws

emblems (EM-bluhmz) Objects or figures that represent another object or idea

flanked (FLANGKT) In battle, to threaten the right or left side of a military formation

formation (for-MAY-shn) A particular arrangement of people, especially soldiers

greaves (GREEVZ) Armor for the knees and shins

mythology (muh-THAA-luh-jee) A collection of traditional tales called myths from a particular culture

outnumbered (owt-NUHM-brd) To have less of something than an opponent

revolt (ruh-VOWLT) A movement to fight against leaders or government

sacrifice (SA-kruh-fise) To give up something to help someone else

Index

Websites to Visit

https://www.britannica.com/event/Battle-of-Thermopylae-Greek-history-480-BC

https://www.historyforkids.net/sparta.html

https://kids.britannica.com/students/article/Sparta/277163

About the Author

Thomas Kingsley Troupe is the author of over 200 books for young readers. When he's not writing, he enjoys reading, playing video games, and investigating haunted places with the Twin Cities Paranormal Society. Otherwise, he's probably taking a nap or something. Thomas lives in Woodbury, Minnesota, with his two sons.

Written by: Thomas Kingsley Troupe
Designed by: Bobbie Houser
Series Development: James Earley
Proofreader: Kathy Middleton
Educational Consultant: Marie Lemke M.Ed.

Photographs:
Alamy: Maximum Film/WARNER BROS.: p. 22-23
Shutterstock: Digital Storm: cover, p. 1; Serhii Bobyk: p. 4-5, 6-7, 18-19, 20; DM7: p. 8; Stasia04: p. 9, 12-13, 24-25; Anastasios71: p. 10-11; Porco_Rosso: p. 14; FXQuadro: p. 15; Kozlik: p. 16; Sonia Bonet: p. 17; immfocus studio: p. 21; Fotokvadrat: p. 26-27; n_ defender: p. 29

Crabtree Publishing

crabtreebooks.com   800-387-7650
Copyright © 2024 Crabtree Publishing

Printed in the U.S.A./072023/CG20230214

Published in Canada
Crabtree Publishing
616 Welland Ave.
St. Catharines, Ontario
L2M 5V6

Published in the United States
Crabtree Publishing
347 Fifth Ave
Suite 1402-145
New York, NY 10016

Library and Archives Canada Cataloguing in Publication
Available at Library and Archives Canada

Library of Congress Cataloging-in-Publication Data
Available at the Library of Congress

Hardcover: 978-1-0398-0948-2
Paperback: 978-1-0398-1001-3
Ebook (pdf): 978-1-0398-1107-2
Epub: 978-1-0398-1054-9